All Rage Blaze Light

Anna Jacobson

Anna Jacobson is an award-winning writer, artist, and researcher from Brisbane (Meanjin), Australia. Her first poetry collection, *Amnesia Findings* (UQP, 2019), won the Thomas Shapcott Poetry Prize. Anna's second illustrated poetry collection, *Anxious in a Sweet Store* (Upswell, 2023), won an Australian Jewish Book Award. *How to Knit a Human*, a memoir, was published with NewSouth in 2024. Anna won the 2020 Nillumbik Prize for Contemporary Writing and a 2018 Queensland Premier's Young Publishers and Writers Award. She holds a Doctor of Philosophy in Creative Writing from QUT for which she received a 2023 Outstanding Doctoral Thesis Award. Anna's poetry chapbook *The Last Postman* (Vagabond Press, 2018) was part of deciBels series 3. She won the 2009 Queensland Poetry Festival Filmmakers Challenge and was a finalist in the Brisbane Portrait Prize, Blake Art Prize, Olive Cotton Award, and Marie Ellis OAM Prize for Drawing. Her website is www.annajacobson.com.au

Endorsements for *All Rage Blaze Light*

Anna Jacobson's *All Rage Blaze Light* is a captivating testament to poetry's ability to revitalise language in a world of brittle meanings and closed-endedness.

With her signature honesty, wit, and craftsmanship, Jacobson's poems shimmer with surprise, energy, and sprightliness.

In this, her latest collection, Jacobson uses the power of poetry to uncover fierce joy and unflinching insight into the human experience.

SIMON TEDESCHI

All Rage Blaze Light is a defiant, incandescent collection that burns through the detritus of psychiatric systems, trauma, and silence to conjure a fiercely imaginative poetics of survival. With searing clarity and surreal lyricism, Anna Jacobson transforms rage into ritual, memory into myth.

Here, trig functions trigger memory, menorahs glow through floodwater, and dreams crack open the psyche with golden thread. Each poem resists erasure—whether through experimental forms, vivid illustrations, or mythic dreamwork—refusing to be silenced by diagnosis or dismissed by institutions.

This is poetry as reclamation: ferociously witty, tender, visionary, and unafraid to blaze.

GAVIN YUAN GAO

In mind. The body. Keep it in mind. The solitude of the five senses? Ergo. Keep in mind what leaves the mind. Offering that goes both ways.

Anna Jacobson gives to you what she has bequeathed herself. Words. Sinew. Synapse. Allow. Try. I could say, but let her!

MTC CRONIN

Anna Jacobson

All Rage Blaze Light

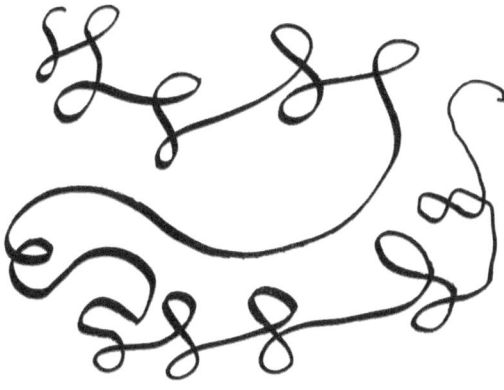

With illustrations by Anna Jacobson

UPSWELL

First published in Australia in 2025
by Upswell Publishing
Perth, Western Australia
upswellpublishing.com

Upswell operates in the city of Perth, on ancient country of the Whadjuk people of the Noongar nation who remain the spiritual and cultural custodians of this beautiful land. We acknowledge their continuing connection to country and express gratitude to elders past and present for their strength and creativity ... Always was, always will be, Aboriginal land.

This book is copyright. Apart from any fair dealing for the purpose of private study, research, criticism or review, as permitted under the *Copyright Act 1968*, no part may be reproduced by any process without written permission. Enquiries should be made to the publisher.

Copyright © 2025 by Anna Jacobson

The moral right of the author has been asserted.

ISBN: 978-0-645-98409-5

 A catalogue record for this book is available from the National Library of Australia

Cover design by Chil3, Fremantle
Typeset in Foundry Origin by Lasertype
Printed by Lightning Source

Upswell Publishing is assisted by the State of Western Australia through its funding program for arts and culture.

Dedicated to Felicity Plunkett, my brilliant mentor,
who shows me how to add fire to my poetry and blaze with light.

Contents

MY FIERY NATURE   13

    My Fiery Nature   15

    Morgiana   16

    Trig Class   18

    Colour Artist   20

    Second and Third Opinion   21

    Magnets Open Walls to Pianos   23

    Trauma's Apprentice   26

    Be the Ocean   29

I NEED THERAPY FROM MY THERAPY   31

    To Do List – Monday   33

    How to Leave Behind Your Psychiatrist of Nine Years   34

    If My Life Were a Dinner Party   36

    Cannot Be Helped   38

    Fragments from a Rainy Thursday   39

    Digging for Agency   40

    Mood Olympics   43

    Mood Ring   45

    Thought Journal   46

    Embodiment Practice: Lesson #1   48

Suggestions from the Distress Tolerance Worksheet	50
Listen to Your Patients	51

MUSEUM OF FLOODS — 53

Museum of Floods	54
Infiltrating Shrinkville	56
How to Make a Home	57
(Orc)hestra	58
How to Want a Home	60
25 Vignettes on the Rental Crisis	61

ORBIT — 69

Galaxy	71
Orbit	72
Chalk Dust and Asteroids	74
Bulk Billing Hours	75
Valley Station Drop Off	77
The Menorah Artists	78
A Pandemic Passover	80
For Chelsea	81
Snail	82
SPAM and the Jewish Consciousness	83
Saturday Art Classes	85
Blue Mask	87

Before I Forget Again	88
Genizah	89
Asher Lev	90
When I Dance	92

MUSEUM OF SYMBOLIC DREAMS   95

EPILOGUE EMBERS   103

Forest	105
Citrine	106
A Season for Everything	107

Acknowledgements   109

MY FIERY NATURE

My Fiery Nature

A psychologist says my fire was taken. After
the session I feel snuffed out, then flare –
my fire is right here, burning. Don't dare tell me
I've turned to ash. Fire's voice speaks
through my body. Fire is my inflammation, pain,
fury. My fire was not taken. I am fire. On fire.
Blazing with its energy. Eating hectares
of psychologists who try to douse me with water –
my fire won't be put out by their words. I whirl
alight, oxidised and flaring, combusting
their practices as damage for their damage.
I transmute my fire to power for patients:
a poetic retribution that won't extinguish,
all rage blaze light.

Morgiana

In my childhood copy of *Ali Baba*
and the Forty Thieves, Morgiana
is my favourite. Once, I read her story
every night. Once, I believed the body
could heal. Skin so miraculous wounds
repair – scars itching with blood
moons, shining cold and hard
on anniversaries.

Instead, I learn the body responds to trauma.
Vertebrae pushed my spine into an 'S'
with the energy stored – my straight
path taken. Trauma led
my lungs to asthma attacks.

So let me be Morgiana, who haunts
on my behalf, dancing with dagger.
Let me be Morgiana, pouring
boiling oil onto forty thieves –
the body is cruel
and my hands burn with anger.

Trig Class

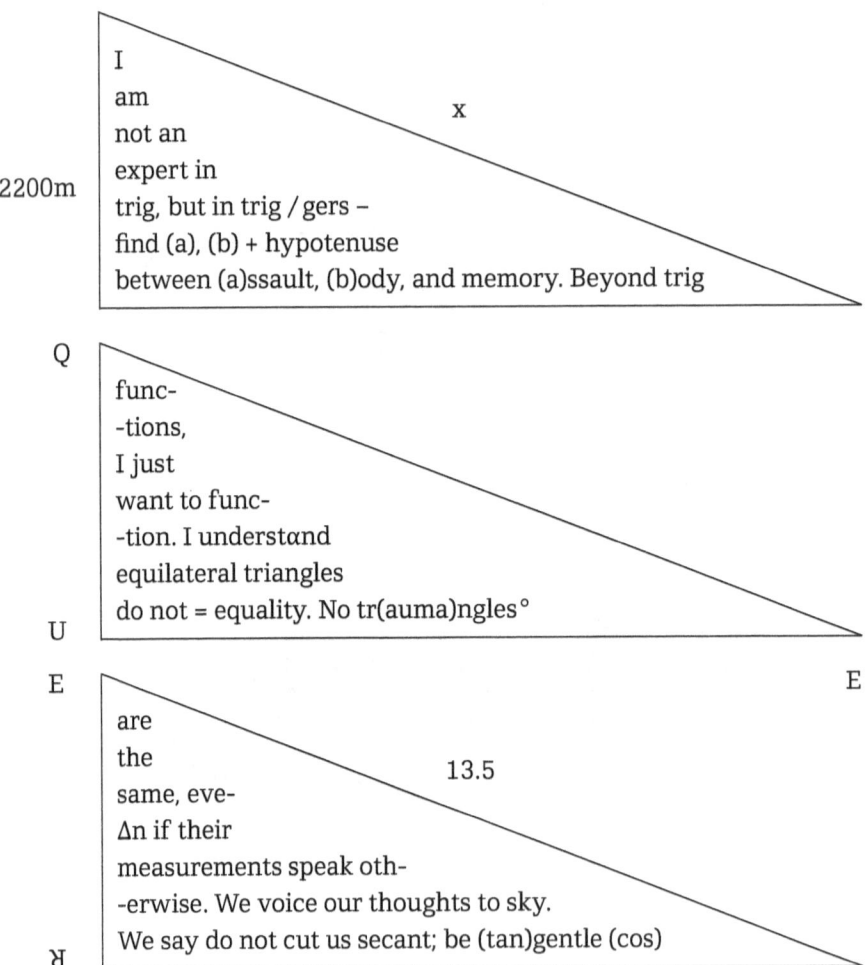

2200m — I am not an expert in trig, but in trig / gers — find (a), (b) + hypotenuse between (a)ssault, (b)ody, and memory. Beyond trig x

Q / U — func- -tions, I just want to func- -tion. I understand equilateral triangles do not = equality. No tr(auma)ngles°

E / Я — are the same, eve- Δn if their measurements speak oth- -erwise. We voice our thoughts to sky. We say do not cut us secant; be (tan)gentle (cos) 13.5 E

we
hθld
sacred
geomet-
-ry inside. We know
how to navigate acute <ang-
-led> experiences. Walk the right /angled\ path, seem-

⟵ 10km ⟶

-ing-
-ly-
oblique.
Scale(ne) vert-
-ical crises. We
learn to reclaim pink triangles,
intersect pride with {spherical} trigonometry

(arc-
-ing)
on all
planes. The last
exercise sees us
pour prosecco on cosecants.
A <u>dash</u> for reciprocal of sine, a <u>dash</u> for us.

Colour Artist

Society agitated my photo-
chemistry, taunted red
safelights, feared exposing
my (photo)sensitivity, tried
drowning me in (stop)baths to halt
further development, washing
me of silver, processing
black and white photographs
from a negative(identity)
they thought was theirs to fix(er)
in place, dodging and burning
to shape my own light.

I escape darkrooms, become
a colour artist, tint with brush on film
by hand. Colour pigments mix
with gum arabic – the brighter
my colours, the deeper
my complexities, the stronger
my self: blues, purples, pinks.
Stars and cosmos weep their jackets off
in joy to see it. These were always
my colours. For the longest time
I didn't know I could paint them
as my own.

Second and Third Opinion

I grieve for my past diagnoses, re-centre
my circumference. Now Anxiety
is Queen. Depression the Duchess.
Complex trauma the Master of the Hunt tearing
me apart every other month.
My bowerbird nest redecorated
with different words, different
shades of blue.

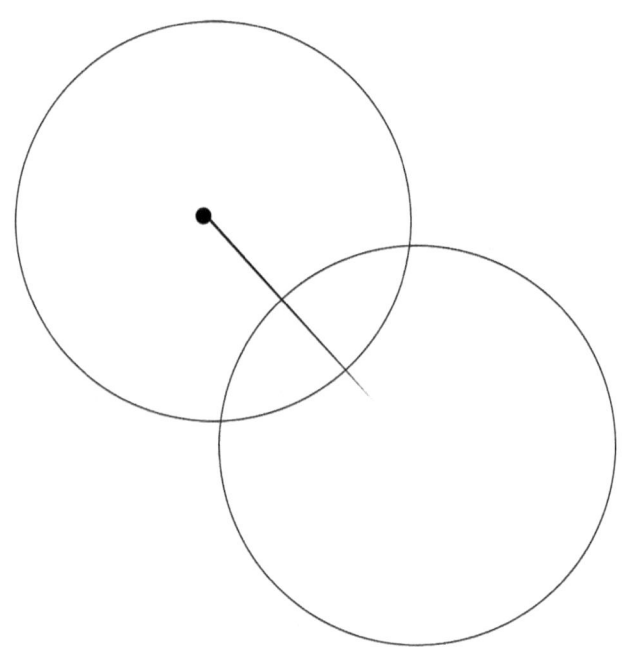

Magnets Open Walls to Pianos

My psychiatrist suggests a course   of Transcranial Magnetic Stimulation
           – says TMS is not like ECT.
Clinicians insist the treatments are 'non-invasive'. Pulsed
                            magnetic
                                    fields placed
over my skull to cause electrical
                        currents in my brain tissue, stimulating
neurons every weekday for twenty minutes   over two months –
does not sound non-invasive to me. I harden
my edges, fold
            myself inside a piano's housing. Heart =
                                      hammering keys,
                          brain =
                              trap work.
My eyes rest on piano's music shelf.
            Notes splay
                    over
                          music desk in staccato
breaths. Rests
        do not exist in this frightening score – do not
tell me to relax as I wait
            for machines to send
                    repetitive beats to restring
alternative futures to my brain's bass
            pedal where wires snap
                    each month. No one sees
or hears as technicians rebuild my trap work. I try
                  not to splint
                          er
            into time
                and space – hold
onto hope

   magnets can retune
        my brain recondition
my body soundboard
      my mood. Doctors say my brain
might perform 'normally' that way.

   Pianos nurse
      the space
        where my voice

        once spoke.

This is a bridge between stanzas – no bridging
        between doctor / patient / system will happen
      in my lifetime.

Magnet pulses crunch
      through coil – my sharp
keys raise of their own facial twitch. Pain
      dumps
in my eye with its metronome dance.
      Retinal injury
is an uncommon risk – the TMS company
      won't proceed
until I see an ophthalmologist. The technicians
are robotic –
      medical trauma reactivates. Technicians
tell me TMS doesn't work
      for some people
      + I am the sum
      of the some.
      88 of my keys
        resisting
          magnetism.

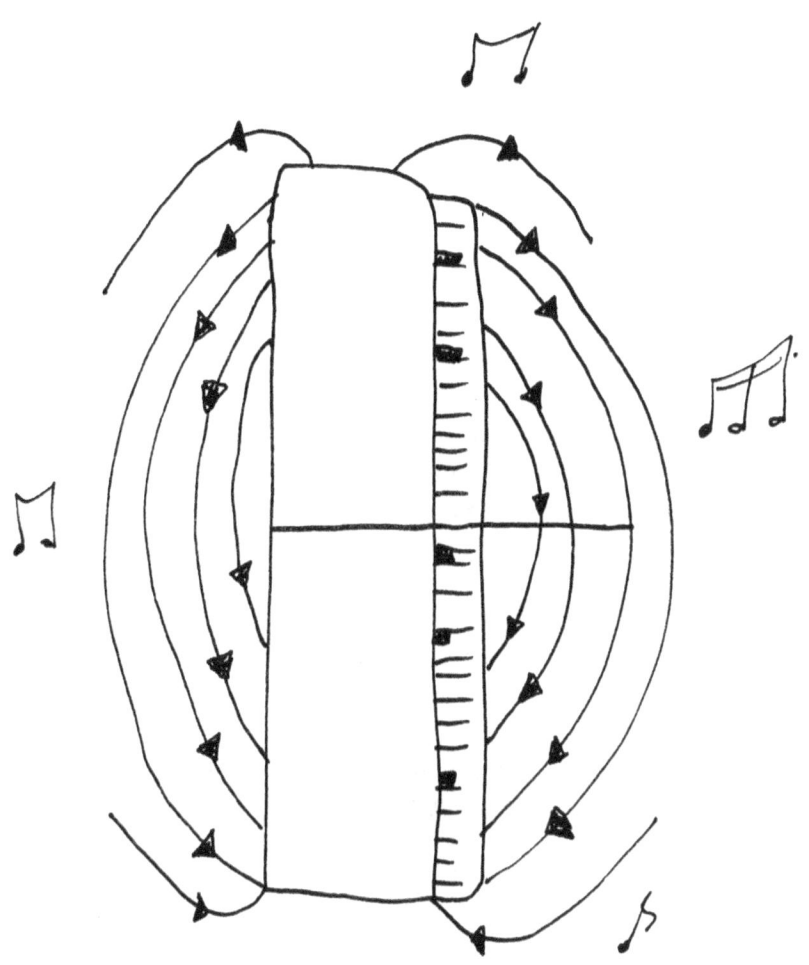

Trauma's Apprentice

What does Trauma look like? You work for her?
That sounds like a long apprenticeship – Passers-by

1.
Trauma is a hundred-year-old woman
with smooth skin. She keeps me busy.
The hours stretch like pulled taffy years.
I get leave from my body. Dissociate. I don't feel
pain. Trauma teaches me how to do this. Now
she is teaching me how not to. How
to notice what my body is feeling. How
my sides squeeze, my chest holds heat,
my jaw clenches, shoulder muscles tense.
Passers-by say I look like I'm in pain.

2.
Trauma has access to my memories.
I'm sick of her hide-and-seek. I am not
a child – sometimes Trauma makes me hurt
like one. She calls me *girl*. I don't know
if I'll ever complete my apprenticeship. Passers-by
say Trauma is from a fairytale, the witch
with sweet tooth and enamelled sugar house.
Sometimes I polish hard-boiled lampposts
until they gleam. I visit with homemade
jam in gingham-wrapped jars when upset.
A potluck offering for two. Sometimes
she is compassionate – we treat ourselves – Portuguese
tart, vanilla slice, scones with tea. Break open jam.
Even Trauma has her own traumas. This doesn't mean
we can't still eat cake.

3.
Trauma tells me I was institutionalised from my trauma.
Trauma was the thread forming
part of the weave. Trauma snowballed
into more trauma, left me in a blizzard
with no clothes, unravelled. Case managers wrenched
open my jaw, forced down breathing exercises,
mindfulness, CBT – snow scarred
my throat. I can't do breathing exercises anymore,
am still wary of psychologists. Trauma nods
as though familiar with the scenario.
Yes, they need to stop telling you how to breathe
while they watch. Say it: Don't tell me
how to breathe. Say it again:
DON'T TELL ME HOW TO BREATHE.

4.
One day Trauma takes me on a field trip.
We float a picnic rug over yellow dandelions.
We are far away from anyone or anything.
How do you feel? I want connection
with other people. Trauma becomes cross.
But you have me! I am teaching
you so many things: empathy, resilience.
I just want to love and be loved. You are making
that impossible. I don't trust anyone. And Trauma says:
You have nearly completed your apprenticeship.

5.
I feel like an old woman, still learning
from Trauma. Trauma is even older now.
Her chicken-feet-hands can't open jars,
fingers scratch at the lids, so I leave
them loose. Passers-by say my apprenticeship
will never end. Trauma says Pain will ebb

and flow: three steps forward, two
steps back. I say I am living my life
as best I can, floating, floating, floating.

Be the Ocean

her body is ancient rock
mineral layers fused
nothing passes trauma's dock

the pelvic physio watches a clock
says, *relax*, bemused
her body is ancient rock

the physio doesn't care, is too ad hoc
ignores painful clues
nothing passes trauma's dock

she reclaims her own body: unlocks
fault lines not her fault – takes refuge
her body was ancient rock

rift valleys sing, turn boulders to clay, a flock
of sands in coloured hues
nothing passes trauma's dock

past breakers she meets another, takes stock –
they could ride its song through blues
her body no longer ancient rock
together they pass trauma's dock

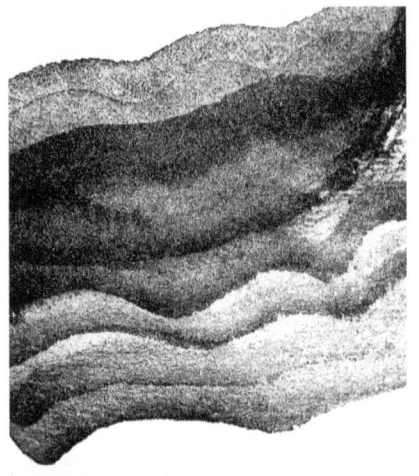

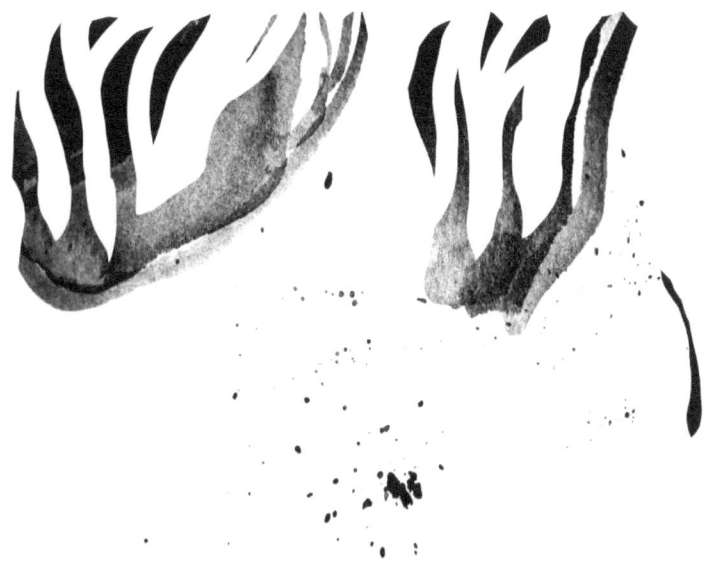

I NEED THERAPY FROM MY THERAPY

To Do List – Monday

- Get out of bed
- Eat breakfast
- Ring new psychology practice to find new psychologist
- Have blood test – non-fasting
- Fill scripts at chemist
- Pay for expensive meds at chemist
- Have lunch special, five dollars cheaper between the hours of 11am – 2pm

How to Leave Behind Your Psychiatrist of Nine Years

Things a psychiatrist said to me:

> *Have you had your pinky toes amputated? Have you heard from your family lately – there was a housefire in their suburb this morning. Are you sure you want to do a PhD – I don't think that's a good idea. My other patients doing PhDs are all in hospital. Don't ever work full time – you're setting yourself up for failure. Are you sure you're bi? Give it six months before telling your family, to sort things out in your own head. If you find driving stressful, why bother? Do you feel normal? Your attitude needs fixing, not the medical system. I may need to put you in community housing. Don't get snippy with me. Practise not attacking those who are trying to help.*

I need therapy from my therapy. Sick
of doctors who make me sick, gaslighting
with so much methane from their collective
four-cow-stomachs they contribute several holes
to the ozone layer. My psychiatrist says:
I've been on this journey with you for nine years.
I think: No, you haven't. You may have been paid
to assess me for forty-five minutes once every two weeks
but you have not lived my experience, felt
my emotions. To claim this is an insult. She drags
out silences – each time I move to speak, she cuts
me off. At the end of the session, for the first
time in nine years she doesn't open the door for me.
I let myself out. I never go back.

If My Life Were a Dinner Party

Last night's dinner eats the table.
She waves away drunken flies –
tongues lick linen tablecloths
for wine stain regrets. Plates balance
like circus acts across the bench.

Candied lemon scatters over half-
torn cakes; evidence of the guests
she's entertained. Lemon peel
sticks to the saucepan with the right amount
of bitterness. She carves potato stamps
with butter knife on raw green spuds.

Her case manager arrives unannounced –
she brews him tea for three minutes,
like the packet says. It smells
of raspberry jelly, stains
the cup deep purple. She reads
the ingredients: rosehip, cherry stems,
blackberry pieces. A free sample delivered
in the mail. Hands the man
a chipped cup with crackers
and dip.

She watches him make his notes. *Dishevelled.*
Averted eyes. Carries potatoes by her side.

The man observes from the door –
she makes notes of her own: *Briefcase filled
with textbooks that do not meet client's needs.
Judgemental. Unworthy
of being a confidant. Presumptive. Ineffectual.*

I'm here to help. Is there anything I can do?
She picks up a potato, presses
it into beetroot dip, stamps
his hand. Glistening
on his palm, the letters N.O.

Cannot Be Helped

She doesn't want to name the five senses.
Doesn't want to squeeze her arm
muscles to ground herself – knows she'd end
in bruises. When her thoughts spike, she doesn't want
to curl her toes, grab the thought, and throw
it away. The counsellor suggests breathing
in a colour, imagining its energy
filling her body as she inhale s   ex   h a   l   es.
This may help some people but not her.
You've gotten this far. You've survived.
What tools have you been using?
Each rough piece hurled in by therapists
she now tosses. Her own tools so finely crafted,
they are invisible to her. She's been seeking
help for over a decade. Her life
feels like a series of consultations, never
getting anywhere. Bad therapists =
𝍷𝍷𝍷 𝍷𝍷𝍷 𝍷𝍷𝍷. Tally = no right fit.

Fragments from a Rainy Thursday

her mind whispers and seethes

speak to yourself
as though you are
speaking to a friend

her mind is not her friend
her mind is not even her

paint a picture for us if you want
an earlier appointment

will her screaming *paint a picture?*
if a picture is worth a thousand words
a scream is surely worth one poem

Digging for Agency

Receptionists eye   me   when I walk
                                        in.
                      When I ask for a glass
      of water.
                    When I pay
for the session. I imagine
                      they note in my file:

Woman arrives three hours early, sobs
in waiting room. Solution: provide vacant
room so as not to scare off other clients.

I note of the receptionists: *Jumpy.*

My new psychiatrist tells me: *If the whites*
                      of your eyes turn yellow, stop
                      taking this med.
If sand begins to pool
          in your ears,
                if you excrete grit tinged the same yellow
      as your eyes,
          stop taking this med.
                        Go to the nearest hospital.
If you feel itchy, stop taking this med also.

        I feel the urge to scratch.

I've spent three months working
            up the courage
      to start a new antidepressant while trying
to survive. Meds marketed at helping anxiety
              are anxiety-provoking. This med is processed

by the liver   where my anger is held – I need blood
tests. The woman at the collection centre doesn't
                                  understand anxiety.
I say no to lying down, refusing
                   until I'm walking through the park
and the world tilts
           its axis – all 365 days.

It's my fifth spin   on the antidepressant wheel:
       the first
               turned my legs to jerk y
wooden puppetry   when crossing the road – I felt
the metal breath   of cars. The last
               whispered I should walk the tracks
               at night.

My past psychiatrist told me to choose
               the next antidepressant. She refused
    to guide me:
said she was worried I'd sue her – handed me
               a stained out-of-date book containing
every type on the market. When I returned
               the book the following week, she acted
               surprised
                   she'd ever given me the book.
               Changeable.

My new psychiatrist says when I'm brave
               enough, I'll try another med,
                   after med,
                   after med.
Brave?   Or self-destructive?
It's been a decade of trying.   I'm not
                   where I want to be
                   with my health –

        maybe it's the meds I've been persuaded
                to take?
    I'm buried
three feet under this side-effect-earth,
        over-medicated, over-monitored
                for a diagnosis that keeps changing. I'm digging
        in the wrong
                direction towards the right therapist.
Ochre-grit yellows
        my itching eyes, chest,
                face.
My mood is plummeting and taking
            me with it.
            My new psychiatrist increases
                    the dose to the highest
                          it will go.

Mood Olympics

Longest world record for:

- Crying
- Most Tried SSRIs

Points for:

- Number of Sacked Psychologists

Gold medal in the *Having to Advocate for Myself
At Every Appointment* category

My Mood Olympics uniform and winnings make it hard
to walk. One hundred medals decorate my neck like weights.
My points earned are floral wreaths I hula hoop around
my arms. My world records are ribbons embossed
with the date and year, streaming behind me like Pin the Tail
on the Doctor. I bear the sash: *It Has Come to My Attention
I Am Traumatised by My Therapists.*

Mood Ring

Domed teardrop set in brass –
a chameleon's eyelid: emerald
to topaz, rose quartz and amethyst.
Colours sans colour chart mellow
to the temperature of my skin.

Thought Journal

Am I standing on train tracks
without realising?

When I tell my psychologist this thought, she says
I lack confidence in my sanity. Either that
or I'm dissociating. I'm in two
places, split –
I'm here, but also on parallel tracks.

I grip metal seats with fingertips, scrunch
toes in shoes, feel concrete. Or
is this a memory? I can only tell
I'm on the platform when trains gloat
past and do not hit. Show me how
to stop my mind from wandering
over yellow lines.

Trust you are on the platform and not
the tracks. It's only a thought. Thoughts
aren't real.

Why do I find psychologists so obtuse?
The psychologists I observe in sessions
are stamped with cookie-cutter edges and inbuilt
markings of refusal to adapt textbook
learnings. Scattering CBT
and 'evidence-based' methods that evidently
do not work for me.

> Show me how
> to 'do the work' when you have not earned
> my trust. Show me how
> to 'do the work' when you show no compassion
> or empathy.

Psychologists offer me stale biscuits
from across train platforms. Crumbs
that help others won't help me.
The biscuits are sprinkled with hundreds
of Milk Duds. I'm sick of duds.
I bake cookies with no edges and chunks
missing, still seeking.

Embodiment Practice: Lesson #1

Trust your gut.

                                                kishke ('kɪʃkə) noun
                                                yiddish: gut

                  I can't trust
                  myself.

Listen to your gut,
notice what you are feeling.

                        Anxiety – my hands are cold.

                                      Cooking with frozen kishke:
                                      a 'how to' guide. Kishke
                                      is a beef intestine stuffed
                                      with flour or matzo meal,
                                      schmaltz, spices – can be added
                                      to cholent.

That's different, keep it separate
to your gut.

                        I don't feel anything then.

                                        I don't need your kick
                                      in the kishkes
                                      to feel pain.

You are out of tune
with your body – you
don't know what your gut
is feeling until you are in pain.

                        Yes.

How can you learn to trust
others when you cannot trust
yourself? When did you last have a gut
reaction?
                It happens with decision-making.

Such as?   Chicken fat or vegetable oil, nu?

                At a cafe the cook put ham
                on my sandwich – I watched
                over the counter. I called out –
                excuse me, no ham, just cheese
                and tomato, please. She removed
                the ham, its juices slick
                over the cheese. She didn't start over
                or remove the cheese but continued to build
                the sandwich. It felt wrong in my gut.

What did you do?
                I ate the sandwich.
                              Why did you not eat kishke
                              instead?

Ahh – you did not speak up
the second time, you did not trust
your gut – first step: notice
what your gut is feeling –
what is your body telling you now?
Yes, no, maybe?
                Maybe.

Maybe is good – maybe is curious.
                The curious kishke gets the final word.

Suggestions from the Distress Tolerance Worksheet

When I say I'm unwell and probably need
to be in hospital, the psychologist says:
*Eat macaroni and cheese! You can cope
more than you think!* When I say there are rocks
in my mouth: *Is it hard candy? I want you to chew
your favourite gum!* When I say I can't stop crying:
Smell the roses! There are no roses
in her sterile office, just warm photocopied pages
from textbook farts. Don't tell me to *Sit
in a new car and breathe the aroma. New cars
make people happy!* Guess what? I don't own a car,
let alone a new one. *Break plates.* My landlord
says I need to be quiet. I shouldn't be left
among broken shards. *Make eye contact
and smile frequently at others!* On my street
that would get me murdered. *Chop
wood.* I don't have an axe or access to a wood pile.
My life isn't *Little Red Riding Hood* unless
you're the wolf. *Well, do something that works
for you.* What works for me is leaving you.

Listen to Your Patients

20 mg
What a helpful side effect. Depressed?
Take this antidepressant – it may unhinge
you further. I'm home from the psych ward
after a med change. Suicidal ideation ignites.
The on-call psychiatrist doesn't listen. His voice,
bitter as escitalopram – I've intruded
on his Saturday. He says: *It's not the meds.*
Says: *This antidepressant is well tolerated
by many.* Says: *It's your 'underlying condition'.*
He ignores black box warnings, convinces me
to increase the dose.

40 mg
I lose my appetite for the first time. Skip
dinner for a month. Withdraw slowly
from the antidepressant while on a waiting list
for a new psychiatrist. My psychologist says
I am making big life changes. My GP says
I need to have a specific goal in mind
for my psychologist. My psychologist says
we can just talk and not have a goal. *We need
to put you on something,* says my new psychiatrist.
I'm already on an antipsychotic – isn't that enough?
How about Valium three times a week?
I've built up a tolerance to benzos.
How about an extra antipsychotic?
Take back your prescription, swallow
your own dose. Don't test my patience.
Listen to your patients.

0 mg

Shrinks say: *Withdrawal symptoms don't exist.*
They like to repeat: *It's your 'underlying condition'
returning.* I say: *Do your research. Undo the harm.*
But there's no Ctrl + Z button in psychiatry
unless Ctrl = CONTROL + Z stands for (Z)oloft.
A past shrink wanted to silence me, Ctrl + Le(X)apro
cut my words after pasting in Ctrl + Lu(V)ox
for a decade. Withdrawal symptoms hold disruptive
year-long parties in my central nervous system,
twanging emotions like slide guitars, sprinkling
sequins into my rice shaker heart. My GP attaches
a Holter monitor to me for a day to Edit-->Find
answers. Suggests I book a sleep study – I can't breathe
at night. Can you interpret my dreams, Mr Technician?
Or do you still see traces of SSRI?

MUSEUM OF FLOODS

Museum of Floods

i.
Water rises through laminate, I pile
belongings, carry objects. Water
cries across floors, beneath bookcases. Four
hours with bucket and mop. Water's
inch – gone. A deluge and in under twenty, sole
deep. I sleep on a couch in the hallway
upstairs. Table's corner, my home.

ii.
The Museum houses thimbles holding
murky water from every flood. Swollen
artefacts lie split at sides, preserved
in lemon. The Museum has space
for each survivor to stay. Mould
does not eat warped doorways.
Glowing in each room: menorahs.
No matter how drenched, light sings.

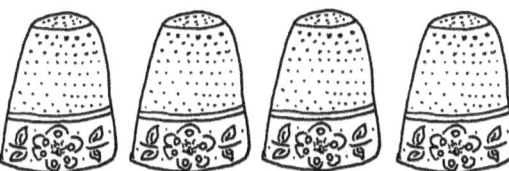

Infiltrating Shrinkville

The street I end up moving
to because of the 2022 February Floods
is Shrinkville – I'm a five-minute walk
from a sepsis of specialists. I rent
on the same street as my psychiatrist's office,
phlebotomists, haematologists, rheumatologists,
near Jacob's Ladder, ascending not to Heaven
but to a demonic compounding pharmacy flaunting
A4 signs: *Please do not disturb the Pharmacist
because we can kill you with one mistake.*
The manager begrudges removing the first sign
when I ask. Refuses to take down the second.
I recover with my favourite meal –
chicken wonton soup at Wicked.

How to Make a Home

Drift rug to floor – the rainbow one
you've carried from rental to rental.
Fill fridge with heirloom
tomatoes. Bring indoor plants you've kept
alive at your old place – lucky bamboo, Devil's
Ivy, a stem of basil to keep
mosquitoes at bay. Rest
these plants on your windowsill. Look
out the window. You are higher
than you've ever lived before. You are in
the city, so close you can hear the clock
tower whose sound reminds
you of your grandparents. Notice
how the clock only chimes between
the hours of 7am and 6pm. Or maybe it sings
longer, thrumming into the workings of your new
rental – here with you, even when it's not. Take
these sounds and furnishings and spell
them into your home. Eat
an heirloom tomato – not red
or yellow, but a magical purple. Taste
your new home through this tomato.
You will settle soon. Soon.

(Orc)hestra

Violence vibrato outside her window – detached
voices, smashing, glass. Panes chime
pavement in musical shatter: bus stop shelters perform
waltzes as car windows splinter into 7/8 time – beaten
in by broken bottles – conductors' batons.
What will she see in the morning?

The city is her nightlight. If she cranes her head
she sees the carpark but not the scene –
musicians dragged across bitumen, thumping
upside-down timpani, laceration of brass
instruments, voices – calm, talking like cello to bass.

Second movement – *tacet*. A car speeds
through the score. She dreams
people light fires outside her building, flames
riff between rests. The warmth of a vigil
as she sleeps.

In the morning, she braces herself, steps outside. Nothing
is out of place. No damage, no shards. Just sounds,
trip-wire-tremolo in her mind.

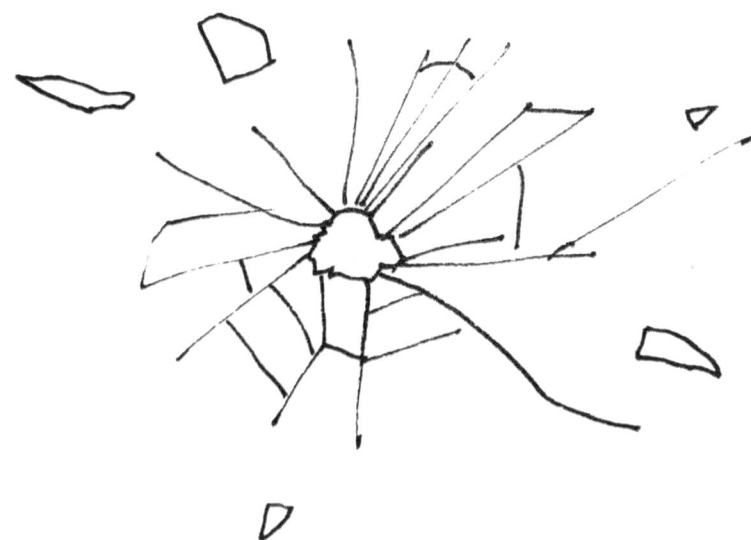

How to Want a Home

At night try not to touch the walls.
Sardine in a subdivided tin,
Listen for the sound of a home – it calls.

At midnight the street laughs wildly, brawls.
Use vinegar on grot – away from linen.
At night try not to touch the walls.

The sponge stains grey and bedside walls crawl.
Move doona from edges, not tucked in.
Listen for the sound of a home – it calls.

Next-door's lover is walking the halls.
He brings hot dhal spiced with cumin.
At night try not to touch the walls.

In the morning the city's sound drawls.
Hear bulldozer's construction.
Listen for the sound of a home – it calls.

Near the building site, mental health falls
into the pit of an industrial bin.
At night try not to touch the walls.
Listen for the sound of a home – it calls.

25 Vignettes on the Rental Crisis

1. When I move into the building, the manager stands in my room. He says it's important for me to be quiet. His gaze fixes on the wall, trying to appease whoever is on the other side.

2. Someone told me that people go missing here – that my street is the Bermuda Triangle of Brisbane. Today was the first day my lips started tasting like metal. I think it's stress.

3. Urgency fizzes the man's voice: *Can you please tell me – is there anything wrong with this building?* I wonder if the man is a journalist or a prospective tenant. He's pulled up on his bicycle, towering over the restaurateur as though trying to intimidate the truth. *You would have to ask the manager,* he says, holding my glance as I pass through sliding doors. There's a tiny sign that reads *this building contains ACM*. I know there is something strange about the building. Tenants in the building are always coming and going, and the open inspections are held on a Sunday. The building is incredibly quiet on a Sunday – deceptively peaceful. Which is why I was surprised after I'd signed the year-long lease to hear construction work starting every morning from 6.30am Monday to Saturday. I cannot think for all the noise of jackhammers.

4. Today the water stopped running and I was left holding an empty cup under the faucet. I phoned the manager, and he said *yes, plumbing works are being done. Should turn on again in ten minutes. Drink plenty of water.*

5. We had a fire drill today. The briefing was held downstairs in the empty restaurant. The woman running the training told us to head down the street if there was ever a fire. *Fire travels uphill,* she says. Tomorrow I will buy a fire blanket.

6. The dryer that came with the rental makes my clothes smell singed after one minute. I've stopped using the dryer. The manager says if I want a replacement, I need to use it until it breaks. I don't want it to catch on fire, so I set up a clothes rack next to the bed. I hang the fire blanket near the dryer.

7. The room I'm renting is in the same street as my psychiatrist's office.

8. When I moved in, there was a patch of dried blood on the floor by the edge of the bed. Perhaps the previous tenant had stubbed their toe on the torn-up base. When I moved the bed to get rid of the clumps of dust, I discovered five Q-tips, cotton-bud heads turned grey. I put on gloves and threw them in the bin. Anything could be in this place.

9. My friends keep telling me that I've got to move out. Find a new rental in a rental crisis. My applications keep being rejected.

10. Fighter jet planes overheard. I can't hear my mother on the phone. Neither of us is being heard against sky's roar. The jets are practising for Riverfire. Feels like the world is ending. *War is coming*, says a barefoot woman holding a long stick. She walks through Roma Steet Parkland in a wraparound dress of grey linen – only I hear her words, louder than my mother's voice against my phone-pressed ear.

11. There's a homeless-looking woman sitting on the pavement next to a sleek black dog. A well-dressed woman pauses mid-stride, says to her husband *what's that beautiful dog doing with the likes of her?* The well-dressed woman hovers as though contemplating calling the authorities to take away the other woman's companion. The green man says go so I go.

12. I see my psychiatrist and tell him about my situation. *Where's your rental?* he asks again. *Around the corner from your office. Up the hill.* Sometimes I think we are both under the same forgetting spell.

13. *People come and go but I've lived here for fifteen years* says penthouse-man at the lifts. An older woman gets in at level three. *Coppers are outside,* she says. On the ground floor I see the street lined with police and ambulances. I go to the park and call a friend. *When are you moving?* she asks.

14. There's no room for a table. I sit on the side-edge of my bed with a bowl balanced on my knees to eat. It's a furnished studio. The mattress that replaced the old one with metal springs poking through has bed bugs which bite, the washing machine is

held together with cloth bandaids and the replaced bar fridge leaks water over my food. Every morning, I take the punnet of strawberries out of the fridge and pour off pooled water from the container lid into the sink.

15. The free loop bus stops right outside the building. There's a permanent security guard on board because of the bus's reputation and history of violence. I'm in the middle section and watch as Security wedges his body between two men – one trying to punch the other. When the bus pulls up to my stop, another girl gets out shaken. I ask if she's okay. She says she's been living in my building for a month. I say I've been here for a year now and she looks at me in awe. The manager still hasn't fixed the aircon in my room and summer is approaching. I don't know whether it's safer to walk home or catch the loop bus anymore. I decide not to go out at night.

16. White powder has started appearing in the grouting and through the cracks in the walls. Maybe it's mould. Or asbestos. My lips still taste metallic.

17. I walk past a pigeon that has fallen from the sky, neck broken and tucked under its wing. I feel it's a bad omen to see a dead animal. I'm superstitious. The last time I saw a severed blue-tongue on a rail pedestrian crossing the floods came, and I had to move out, find a place quickly. Ended up here.

18. I wake with pain in my hands. The air in my room smells of crushed dust and plaster from the construction site. I can see particles in the morning light.

19. I attend a rental inspection that takes over an hour of travel to find. The agent is on the phone nearby. The current tenant smokes outside on the balcony. *Does it come with a washing*

machine and fridge? I ask. *It can. I can sell you mine.* He exhales smoke into the flyscreen. *No room for a dining room table,* says a woman who is looking on behalf of her daughter. *It's small,* says another. To me, this place feels huge. But it's opposite a petrol station that is so new it hasn't shown up on the map. I can smell the fumes from outside the building. *Did you enjoy living here?* I ask the tenant. *It's quiet,* he says. I know he is lying – there must have been a year of construction work and drilling into the foundations to build the new petrol station.

20. The next rental I inspect has no security screens. *Do you know if there is construction noise in the area?* I ask the agent. The agent pauses. *No, I don't know.* In her pause I remember I have passed a construction site only a block away.

21. I get in late from my graduation. I unwrap the frame I've ordered for my PhD testamur and place the parchment inside. I turn out my light and get into bed. The man in the studio next door waits until the night settles then whispers through the walls: *You woke me up, you stupid cunt.*

22. I am heading out of the building to get my hair cut. When the lift doors open, there is a man leaning against the inside of the lift. He looks like he is having an upright seizure. He isn't wearing a shirt but is wearing shorts. A single pair of underpants is twisted on the floor. I stand in the corridor, staring, unable to move as the lift doors automatically close themselves again. I take the stairs. I figure the man needs help and might be having a drug overdose. I've never seen someone having a drug overdose before. I ring the manager and tell him that I think the man needs medical attention. The manager says: *I'll keep it in mind.* When I get back from my appointment, the lift is empty, underpants removed.

23. My doorknob rattles and rotates. Second time in two months. Someone is trying to get into my room and is testing my door to see if it will open. I don't feel safe. If I don't find another place to live, the building will eat me alive.

24. I ring a helpline. I want to remain anonymous. *We like to leave a name with the notes, so you don't have to repeat yourself next time.* Call me Fire Girl.

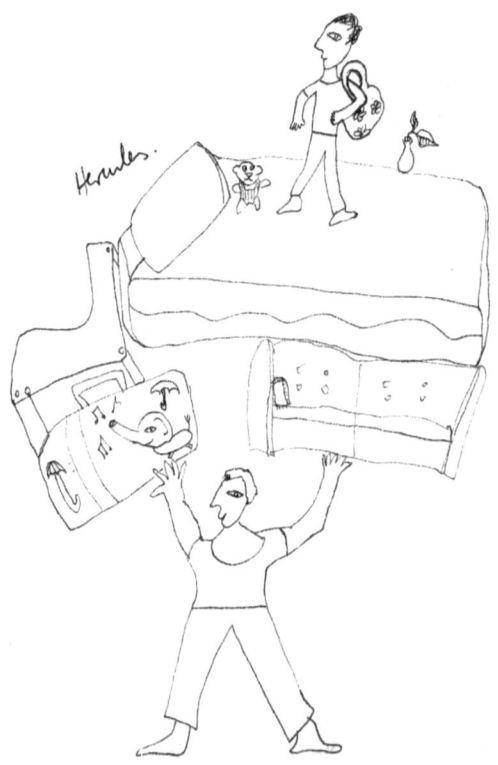

25. Hercules moves my gear into the lift and down to the carpark as the building's occupants watch on. After one-and-a-half years I've been accepted for a new rental. The one-bedroom apartment is nearly double the amount of rent per week than the old room

but with the new job payslips, I can finally be considered for a place with flyscreens, a kitchen, and secure 24-hour swipe access to the building. Somehow, Hercules single-handedly carries the bed up three flights of stairs and into the apartment. He twists the legs off the second-hand couch, so it fits through the door. *Your bathroom here is the whole size of your old place*, says Hercules before he leaves for his next job. I decorate with bright, patterned fabrics and cuttings of Devil's Ivy in water vases. My lucky bamboo has finally brought me luck. There's an op shop down the street where I find a three-tiered plant holder, retro cookie jar, ceramic plates, and glass teapot. Palm trees rustle outside my window, letting in so much natural light I don't need to flick a single switch.

ORBIT

Galaxy

Elbow silver buttons at pedestrian lights,
sticky moons like spoons holding crushed
meds in honey. I never wanted meds –
pink white yellow blue. Popped
from foil crinkle, sealed
plastic lids, a rustling sachet
for freshness – do not eat
the sachet, but inappropriate meds
are just as dangerous.
I leave my room, find
my favourite tree, search
for places where my voice
is heard – where stars
outshine the moons.

Orbit

Grief is a feeling that orbits my body. Sometimes
the centre of gravity changes and new orbits form
around my head heart soul. Sometimes the orbits
go through me, circumnavigating my solar plexus.
Once I buried Grief under a mango tree. Once I flew
with Grief in a light aircraft, soaring so high I saw
the arc of the world. Once I was told to sit with Grief.
It wasn't very good company. Grief made me cry.
I told it to go. It wouldn't shift track.

Chalk Dust and Asteroids

I breathe night's seams
river-streets flex eels   sound
waves echo my walk's blue
              current
this time a circle   a purple-eyed
           moth
bass drum chews bubblegum
hips pop pride confetti
                dance
dance   spacewalk the stars

Bulk Billing Hours

The taxi driver can't find the address.
Says: *This is all I know – it's 100 metres
from here.* The carpark is alien-landscape-
eerie. I follow the yellow line for after-hours
access. Press the intercom. A voice says
if I can't open the door there's nothing
she can do – that I'll have to go the long
way round.

What's the long way?

The intercom shuts off. Maybe
she thinks I'm staff. Maybe I am
trying to get through the wrong door
that says: *For staff and security only.*
All signs have led me here. I wrench
the door that doesn't want
to come free, pulling
so hard the frame shakes and rattles
open. A security guard finds me wandering
the hallways of an abandoned hospital –
all info desks are devoid of staff.

Can I help you?
I'm looking for the X-ray building.
They open this late?
Bulk billing hours.
He nods, says: *Follow me.*

The X-ray building is outside
on the street, tucked
into a side carpark nowhere

near where the taxi dropped me. Bulk
billing hours are for those who can't
afford expensive MRIs. The system
makes us pay another way. Demands
we scuttle through midnight when the world
roughens its edges, offers
us up as bait.

Valley Station Drop Off

for Aaron and his Jag

In the hour-and-a-half before midnight we crest
the hill in our cousin's old Jag. A butcher, blood
on white apron, haunts the sidewalk. A man in a cape
hoists a caution-floor-is-wet bollard onto shoulders,
wedges it through the open window of the car
ahead. Our cousin swings into the drop-off zone
where butcher dances with her knife. *Nice Jag*
says the butcher's friend. *Do you want to be scared?*
My brother says: *No thanks*, his voice calm
and measured in time to the sleek grand piano
being ballad-played by an untouchable pianist. Inside
the station, eleven Super Marios steamroll our way.
A police officer tells two men in skeleton-bone
jumpsuits they need ten dollars for their journey. Below
on the platform all is quiet. An attendant pulls up a man
for stepping on the yellow line.

The Menorah Artists

The menorah I took
into the psychiatric ward – silvery
plastic with battery
-powered lights. Blue-bright,
even when Nurse knocked
over my flower vase, water splashing
the base. Staring at its light without
my glasses – better than Valium.

My childhood menorah –
brass, each holder a figure
carrying candle flame. The spare
menorah – a sculptured tree of silver, each
branch a nest for candles. Grandma's
gifted menorah – layered with stones.

The menorah I once made at Cheder –
a plank of wood with golden bottle
caps for the eight candles and an extra
for the Shamash. The emergency
menorah I found in a gift shop away
from home – wrought iron. Candle wax leaks
through holders meant
for ornamental use only.

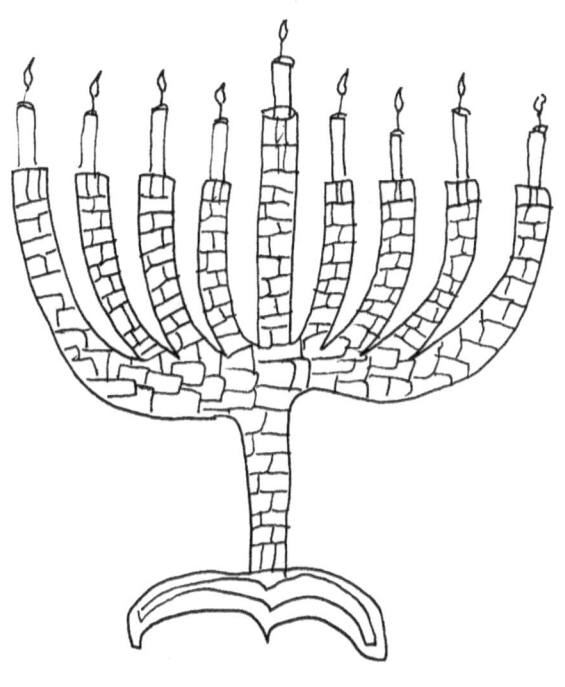

A Pandemic Passover

I can't visit
        my family, try
not to cry
       into my Thai
takeaway, lamb shank curry on the bone –
the closest I could get to Z'roa
on the Seder plate. For an orange
all I have is a pithy mandarin.
No shred of bitter
herb, no flame to roast
an egg, or karpas to dip
into my salt
water tears.
I can't find
a single box of matzah
in Brisbane – from the vegan
store I buy rice
thins – taste worse than cardboard
Shmurah matzah, Styrofoam.
The Pandemic has eaten my Passover.
Shrunken my experience like the tightening
skin of this old mandarin under fingernails.
I do not read from the Haggadah or say
prayers. I do not drink four cups of wine
or lean to the left. I say to myself: *Next year
with my family*, curl up in bed
early, like a piece of stale chametz.

For Chelsea

We find heart-shaped biscuits, sprinkled
in sugar. I'll have the broken one, I say.
No, have the best one.
Her seven-year-old eyes pick me out
a perfect golden heart.

Snail

After Sunday School, my friend
holds a jar of glitter, shimmer-fine.
Tells me her grandparents collect
silvery dust from the magick paths
of snails. Gifts for her spells
and wishes. I know not to ask for any.
My friend dips her smallest finger
in silver, anoints my temples, says:
Make a wish.

SPAM and the Jewish Consciousness

I travel from Brisbane
to Canberra for year 7 camp,
to learn about politics.
Everyone is hungry.
No one can eat the SPAM.

No ham on my form.
SPAM served
from radioactive blue tins. Ask
for the vegetarian option.

The vegetarian meal has been taken,
says the cook. *Here* – a scoop
of watery peas. Two potatoes, size
of shrivelled dates.

Can I please have more potatoes, then?
Two potatoes each.
My friends, horrified,
give me their potatoes –
golden eggs. *Tell the teachers,*
they say but I can't.

Later I find out another girl
had taken the vegetarian option –
a tuna patty. I don't mind she ate
my meal, am surprised
she's never told me about being Jewish.

Perhaps far from home she wanted
to be more kosher that night. I understand
how culture can weave in and out

of consciousness. Spring up
when least expected like a storm
lily after rain.

Saturday Art Classes
for my art teachers

Listen to ghost stories near paint
and brushes. Draw stippled demons
in charcoal, glue-gun twine. Block
print fabric. Pick berries, seeds, twigs
from artists' gardens. *Collage these
ingredients. Can't sew? Nonsense! Here –
take needle, thread, potato sack.* Awaken
from art-realms to eat iced cake with paint-
stained fingers. Hold
onto art – these pieces of self, all
the way home.

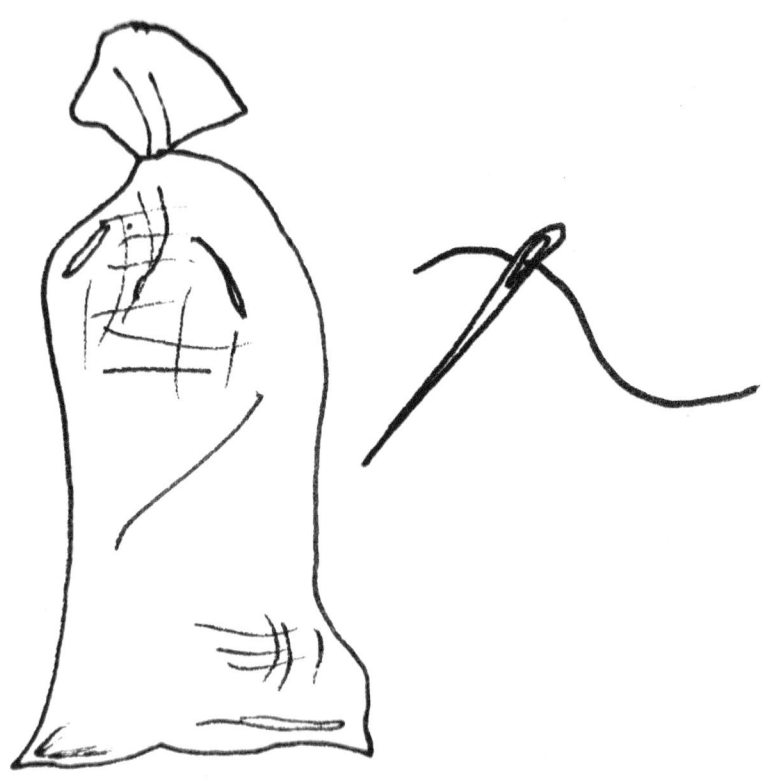

Blue Mask

Swirl glue, edge mask's eyes golden. Glitter
glimmers indigo feathers. Azure
wishing stone obscures a third
eye. I hold my papier-mâché mask
as a dybbuk unfurls within – a spirit
who takes possession, turns
me Other. If only the dybbuk had lodged
in my smallest toe and not my third
eye, masking myself from my self.

If I'd salted the corners of my room, with extra
left over for pockets' seams – a walking Dead
Sea art installation – the dybbuk might have cracked
the windowpane as it left. But with the dybbuk
wedged in the wishing stone of my third
eye, I could not see for all the glass, until
I could again.

Before I Forget Again

After Julie Field's 'Signed Planet Earth'

I am a ceramic horse in kintsugi
fields. Shards shred my tongue to gold
rivers. Cracked and crazed – from fire
gallops beast. Memory slips
lapis lazuli. I break
curses, gather spells. Nudge
fresh letters in water
troughs – watch each word bob – shiny
new apples to crunch.

Genizah

1.
I want to dream of a genizah – all curved archways and pillars. Inside this hiding place where damaged but sacred books are stored, I want to explore fragments and scraps from falling-apart pages. Spend hours in their company, before their tender burial with the rabbi's kaddish. I know where the genizah in my synagogue is kept. Do not know where the genizah in my mind is kept – perhaps the memories are no longer needed or were long ago torn and tucked away in the amygdala, whose name reminds me of the weekday Amidah. I step into the prayer – take three steps forward and three steps back.

2.
I dream I am admiring a dress I wore as a young child. A blue and white dress with soft scalloped collar and zigzag ruching lying out of place, on a table in a genizah. I know the dress will be buried respectfully in the ground. I yearn for the fabric but am resigned to its burial. I move on to another room.

Asher Lev

At fourteen I leafed
through your world. Chaim Potok created
you and now your character stays.
Asher Lev, I am free
to make art; encouraged, even.
You are my Jewish hero – but full
of suffering, Asher Lev. You fought
for every brushstroke. I wanted to analyse
your works in my art assignments –
they must exist somewhere, apart
from my mind. I wanted to be you
when I was younger.

I found a book in the art
library – *Complex Identities: Jewish Consciousness
and Modern Art*, felt recognised, ordered it
from a bookshop. I bought this
for myself; a book not already on my parents'
shelf, and I thought of you, Asher Lev –
you did not have these kinds of books
or know others like you. And in another time
or place, I may have been you, fighting
to create, shunned
for expression. I took art
classes on the Sabbath.
And what I am trying to say, Asher Lev,
is that I am lucky to have support
from my family and community
to create art and write. I am lucky, I am
lucky, I am lucky.

When I Dance

My body is made up
of bent coathangers. I'm a statue
fixed at the hips. A rough
music translation to a score I once knew
by instinct.

Trauma's shoes look like this: enmeshed
sinews and ligaments, starting at feet.
Not easy to take off. All connected – a root system.

I once saw a man crossing Brisbane streets –
his bare feet and legs trickled watery blood. I hold
his image – think: *This
is what would happen if I ripped
off trauma's shoes.*

I buy a pass to an inclusive dance class.
And another. Some nights I twirl. Watch
shadows sway. No longer floating-stuck.
Relearning my body's language – this slow dance
with myself. Some nights I am still
a coathanger statue. Some nights
I have trouble transcribing
my body's music. Other nights
a cat dances in my chest – and I
                                   dance with her.

MUSEUM OF SYMBOLIC DREAMS

The rabbi speaks of messages in dreams that the soul hears but the body doesn't. To listen to the spirits when they try to reach you. My dreams are puzzles to unwrap on waking. I place dozens of Dream Dictionaries on hold. They wend their ways from six different libraries, arriving all on the same day. Lug them home in a peacock bag flung over my shoulder. One book says that during times of stress, dreams are more vivid.

The museum is closing for lunch. Whatever room we end up in, we will have to remain for the hour. The doors are slowly closing. Find myself in the cicada room – a richly patterned wallpapered room with a giant cicada sculpture. I am alone, with one other. The cicada is a symbol of transformation and growth. Feel hopeful for my day ahead, and my future.

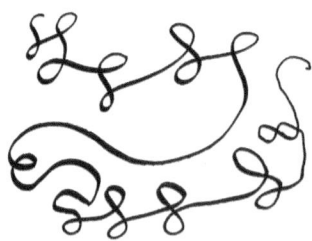

I dream golden thread is painted on my face, body, and walls of the gallery in an installation by an artist – a young woman unknown to me but who seems familiar. The thread is connected in one long swirling line, glimmering, and glittering from the soft-haired brush. Art installations of unbroken golden thread: repairing through hard work and patience, creativity, self-expression, and luck.

Bubbling toxic carpet. Holes eat their way into the floor of my bedroom. Caterpillars crawl around the holes. There is a lime on the floor. The clothes on my body fall off me in strips, as though cut with scissors. When I check the time, the watch face shows twelve wriggling blue hands. Twelve wriggling blue hands in the presence of cut clothing and limes: desire for change and balance during difficulties, as cycles begin and end. The dream is telling me I am about to go through my next transformation.

I'm riding a bicycle barefoot to the park at night. So tired, I lie down on a bench near a group of boys who are talking quietly. Wake on the bench with my childhood doona cover over me, the one with all the French shopfronts and flower stalls and ice-cream shops. The group has gone, and all my possessions are still with me. I am unharmed. In fact, I now have shoes. Bare feet on a bike: an exposed journey requiring the dreamer's effort. Shoes near childhood doona cover: protection for the dreamer as they continue onwards.

A letter has reached me from a woman called Perl. She wants to catch up and has moved to my suburb. The post office has passed my address on to Perl without my permission. Perl seems okay – though I recall she had lots of problems, and I don't really want to be in contact with her, which is why I moved in the first place. I wonder who Perl represents in my dream. But I already know the answer. Perl is probably me. I am trying to run from my self.

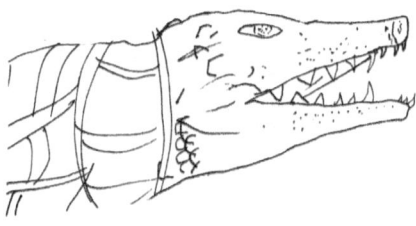

Giant crocodile the size of five lions is tied up in grey knotted ropes, suspended under the surface of a lake. My task is to scrub my swimwear clean, then venture underwater to see it. A crocodile tamer floats nearby to make sure the crocodile does not escape. The creature is becoming aggravated, its head free of the ties. The crocodiles in my dreams are moving closer. Crocodiles in grey ropes: hidden dangers and emotions. The dreamer may be undernourished. Cleaning of clothing: to cleanse and protect oneself from burdened memories. Confronting the crocodile: a wish for shared knowledge.

My friend turns into one of my worry dolls. I rescue her from the bottom of a bowl of soup, and she turns back into a person. Worry Dolls in soup: comfort and healing is required.

Flames vanish from the windows of a house but reappear when I look through a mesh window screen. Vanishing flames through a window screen: the dreamer is learning lessons around emotional patterns.

My friend is making cards for everyone – mine features a Leviathan sticker. She tells me to position it on the card myself. I line up each pointed tooth with her stencil. Lightning writhes on the ground in thick swirling bolts. Of Leviathans and lightning: fear and immense challenges. Epiphanies and spiritual new paths.

Searching to speak to my psychiatrist. Multiple inner doors. They are white and unmarked – I push them open from the middle. They split to let me pass. Opening an unmarked door with no handle: transitions and new opportunities – something positive is about to unfold.

|

I want to free ghosts, but a wall blocks me. Each ghost is housed in a suitcase, art folio case, or between sheets of cardboard. I am trying to carry them all to the other side of the wall. Ghosts in suitcases before a wall: attempting to carry unresolved remnants into the present that are being protected.

|

Spitting miniature bells out of my mouth that keep multiplying beneath my tongue. When I hold a tissue to my lips, I see watery blood. Spitting silver bells with blood: communication with spirits calling the dreamer to action. Transference of energies from waking world to dream. The dreamer is reaching their limits.

|

Three people walk through a door I haven't noticed before on the left-hand side of my room. When they leave, I get out of bed and latch all extra doors that allow others to enter. Only then do I discover the other rooms. I seal up the rooms again, though now I have seen I cannot unsee. The wide window to one of the rooms remains open despite the door being closed. A private balcony sprawls with a garden I hadn't known was there. Some plants are yellowed, others green and thriving. My dream-self plans to use the balcony and nurture the garden. Number three on the left: the untried melding of spirit, body, mind. Locking doors: protecting unconscious selves. Extra rooms: rediscovery of lost selves. Closed door open window: obstacles among hope. Garden: inner beauty, creativity.

My hairdresser is driving me through the suburbs to fix my hair. The car falls onto a piece of bitumen hovering above a rainforest. We are stuck, but he gets us out again. Car: self-discoveries. Hairdresser: a guide to the present. Rainforest: inner selves gifting ecosystem skills.

Yellow leaves twirl in spiritual breeze. I'm choosing where to stage my play – the old amphitheatre is overgrown with grass. I pick this outdoor space. Amphitheatre: wanting to be seen and heard. Overgrown: need for care. Falling leaves: letting go for new knowledge.

I'm driving a colossal golden truck so big it's a moving mountain. I can see all the landscapes from here. The truck is in beautiful condition. Big golden truck in beautiful condition: spiritual illumination through confidence and personal knowing. The dreamer is on the right path.

EPILOGUE EMBERS

Forest

There is an ancient forest that no one can harm –
and it has lived inside me for longer than I have existed
on this earth.

Citrine

For Ash

My hairdresser gifts me a Citrine for my birthday. The quartz appears glittering and golden in his palm like magick. He tells me it will protect me with its healing properties – to carry the crystal in my bag or pocket and cleanse her in the full moon. To rid the self of unwanted energy, smudge with fire.

A Season for Everything
For Peter

My search ends at a treehouse in the frangipanis around the corner from my home. As soon as I hear his voice, I know I'm in safe hands. He's different from the others. Transparent, letting me see his thoughts as though sharing a bowl of handwritten stones. He lets me pick one and I hold it in my palm. This therapist gives back when I speak – radiates insights and woven responses. Gifts of perspective told simply. He asks the right questions. Tells me I've needed to be my own therapist for so long; that I've already done much of the work through my writing and art. The Chevra Kadisha – burial society of my mind – strips my past of its clothes and covers me in a white sheet, a fresh notebook for new beginnings. I trust like I've never trusted before. Envisage how I want my future to look. Finally, it is my time to heal. We sit across the room from one another. Intimacy in this close-listening distance. His presence with me as compassionate as the Tahara – the washing of the dead – bringing me back to life. He asks me if each part of my self wants to be here. When I say *yes*, he tells me auspicious words I need to hear that make me sit up, goosebumps of hope prickling my arms. My therapist looks me in the eyes and says: *there is a season for everything. And that season is coming. Don't rush.*

Acknowledgements

This book was written in Brisbane (Meanjin), Australia. I would like to acknowledge the Traditional Custodians of the land on which I live, write, work, and create – the Jagera and Turrbal people, and pay my respects to Elders past and present.

I am thankful to have such beautiful family and friends whose love, support, and encouragement has seen me through difficult times. Friends who I especially want to thank during this period in my life are Nadia Myers, Charlotte Brakenridge, Anne Sawyer, Ellen van Neerven, Nathan Shepherdson, Pascalle Burton, Simon Tedeschi, Bernard Cohen, Peter Wilson, Rebecca Smith, Bronwyn Lacken, Gavin Yuan Gao, Heidi Stevens, Phoebe McDonald, Tammy Vu, Hui Li, Rae White, Kris Kneen, David Cohen, Carly-Jay Metcalfe, Bec Davis, Raelee Lancaster, and J.R. Thank you also to my incredible hairdresser and friend, Ash.

I have many special people who I consider to be lights and guides in my life, and for this book, there is one writing mentor, friend, and editor I would especially like to thank for showing me how to add fire to my poetry and blaze with light. That person is Felicity Plunkett, to whom this collection is dedicated. Felicity gave generous, gentle, kind, and intuitive feedback on my poems, which helped me shape my collection. Her light gives me courage, and hope. And to my new therapist, Peter – the healing journey with you is transformational. Thank you for your compassion, generosity, and care.

Thank you to the marvellous Terri-ann White at Upswell, for publishing *All Rage Blaze Light*. Thank you to Kelly Lee for her clear proofreading, and to Keith Feltham for typesetting this collection, including navigating my poems with experimental formatting and illustrations. Thank you to Becky Chilcott from Chil3 for matching the background golden ochre shade to my artwork on the cover design.

An earlier version of *All Rage Blaze Light* was shortlisted in the 2023 Helen Anne Bell Poetry Bequest Award. Thank you to the judges, editors, and publishers of the poetry journals, anthologies, commissions, and opportunities where earlier versions of poems from this collection first appeared. 'Museum of Floods' was published in the *Resilience* anthology (Ultimo Press, 2022). 'Colour Artist' was exhibited in *Dear Queensland* at QAGOMA. 'Asher Lev' was published in *Rabbit* poetry journal's Art issue. 'Second Opinion' was published in *Australian Poetry Journal*, and 'Before I Forget Again' was published in *Griffith Review*. 'If My Life Were a Dinner Party' was exhibited as 'Potato Stamp' at the 2017 National Young Writers Festival, as a finalist in the *Phone It In* Story Phones installation. My poem 'Orbit' was composed into a piece of music by cellist Katherine Philp and performed as part of *When We Speak* at the 2022 Brisbane Music Festival.

An earlier version of 'Listen to Your Patients' was commissioned by Red Room Poetry for MAD Poetry 2021 and was published in *A Line in the Sand: 20 Years of Red Room Poetry* (Pantera Press, 2023). My video recording of this poem featured during Mental Health Week in partnership with Survivors of Suicide & Friends and Red Room Poetry. 'Chalk Dust and Asteroids' was published in *Jacaranda Journal*. An earlier version of '25 Vignettes on the Rental Crisis' was longlisted in the 2024 Gwen Harwood Poetry Prize, published in *Island* online on World Poetry Day, and shortlisted in the 2024 Poetry Category of the Woollahra Digital Literary Award.

My section 'Museum of Symbolic Dreams' draws on my 2024 Dream Diary. I acknowledge the Dream Dictionaries I consulted for prompts on symbolism as inspiration for my meaning-making, in my own words: *Llewellyn's Little Book of Dreams* by Dr Michael Lennox (2017, Llewellyn Publications); *The Dictionary of Dreams: Every Meaning Interpreted* by Linda Shields (2017, Wellfleet Press); *The Dream Dictionary from A to Z* by Theresa Cheung (2006, Thorsons); *The Complete A to Z Dictionary of Dreams* by Ian Wallace (2014, Vermilion); and *The Dictionary of Dreams* by Gustavus Hindman Miller, Sigmund Freud, and Henri Bergson (2017, Wellfleet Press).

While there are multiple interpretations for any one object or symbol, I transform these meanings to my specific dreams, intuitive feeling, and personal associations. Dreams and dream work are often seen as an important activity for spiritual connection in Jewish tradition, and the importance of dreaming varies across different cultures. This section continues my interest in symbolic dreams and how the unconscious mind can process meaning from experiences, emotions, and thoughts into objects that appear outside our awareness in the waking world but are revealed to each dreamer in the dream world. I look at symbolic dreams from a place of curiosity for personal understanding and comfort. For me, dreams are clues and puzzles to unwrap on waking.

About Upswell

Upswell Publishing was established in 2021 by Terri-ann White as a not-for-profit press. A perceived gap in the market for distinctive literary works in fiction, poetry and narrative non-fiction was the motivation. In her years as a bookseller, writer and then publisher, Terri-ann has maintained a watch on literary books and the way they insinuate themselves into a cultural space and are then located within our literary and cultural inheritance. She is interested in making books to last: books with the potential to still be noticed, and noted, after decades and thus be ripe to influence new literary histories.

About this typeface

Book designer Becky Chilcott chose Foundry Origin not only as a strong, carefully considered, and dependable typeface, but also to honour her late friend and mentor, type designer Freda Sack, who oversaw the project. Designed by Freda's long-standing colleague, Stuart de Rozario, much like Upswell Publishing, Foundry Origin was created out of the desire to say something new.

www.ingramcontent.com/pod-product-compliance
Lightning Source LLC
Chambersburg PA
CBHW030223170426
43194CB00007BA/839